School
In Grandma's Day

by Valerie Weber
and Gloria Jenkins

Carolrhoda Books, Inc./Minneapolis

Carolrhoda Books, Inc., A Division of the Lerner Publishing Group
241 First Avenue North, Minneapolis, MN 55401 U.S.A.

Website address: www.lernerbooks.com

Planning and production by Discovery Books
Edited by Faye Gardner
Text designed by Ian Winton
Illustrations by Stuart Lafford
Commissioned photography by Sabine Beaupré and David Wright

The publishers would like to thank Gloria Jenkins for her help in the preparation of this book.

Library of Congress Cataloging-in-Publication Data

Weber, Valerie.
    School in grandma's day / Valerie Weber and Gloria Jenkins.
        p.   cm. — (In grandma's day)
    Includes index.
    Summary: Recalls what it was like to go to both a public and a Catholic school in Illinois in the 1940s.
    ISBN 1-57505-327-6 (alk. paper)
    1. Jenkins, Gloria, 1937–   . —Childhood and youth—Juvenile literature.   2. School children—Middle West—Social life and customs—20th century—Juvenile literature.   3. Elementary schools—Middle West—History—20th century—Juvenile literature.   4. Catholic elementary schools—Middle West—History—20th century—Juvenile literature.   5. Middle West—Social life and customs—20th century—Juvenile literature. [1. Schools—History—20th century.   2. Catholic schools—History—20th century.   3. Jenkins, Gloria, 1937–   —Childhood and youth.]
I. Jenkins, Gloria, 1937–   . II. Title.   III. Series: Weber, Valerie. In grandma's day.
LA229.W395   1999
370'.977—dc21   98-2824

Printed in Hong Kong
Bound in the United States of America
1 2 3 4 5 6 - OS - 04 03 02 01 00 99

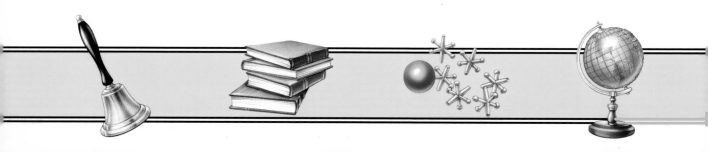

Contents

School in the 1940s

My name is Gloria Jenkins. I was born in 1937 in Peru, Illinois, and went to grade school during the 1940s. I have five grandchildren and eight step-grandchildren. You can see me here with Jennifer, who is seven; Taylor, who is four; Sammy, who is three; and Noah, who is just three months old.

From 1941 to 1945, the United States fought in a war called World War II. Both my parents worked in jobs that were necessary for the war. My dad, who was Polish American, butchered meat for the soldiers to eat. My mother, who was Yugoslavian American, worked for four years at a factory like the one in the photograph on the left. The factory made guns, bullets, bombs, and grenades for the war.

Once, a woman at the factory dropped a tray of grenades, which blew a hole in the floor. My mom quit the factory that day and went to work at a factory that made different kinds of clocks for the war effort.

While my parents were at work, I went to school. In some ways, school in the 1940s was like the school you go to. It was different in other ways. Let's see how.

My First School

From kindergarten through second grade, I attended a public school. It was in a new red brick building that was named the Roosevelt School, after President Theodore Roosevelt. All the classrooms were on one floor. It looked like the school in the picture below. It had a great playground with swings, slides, and a baseball backstop, which is the fence behind the batter.

I walked over two miles to the public school, crossing a busy highway by myself with no crossing guard. There were only crossing guards, usually seventh or eighth graders, at the corner nearest the school.

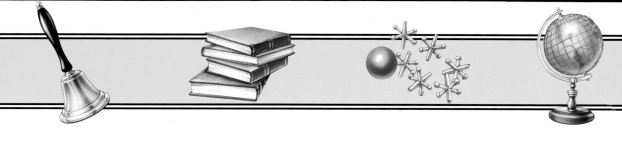

There were fifteen children in my kindergarten class. The picture below, taken in front of my school, shows only ten of my classmates because the others were out sick that day. I'm third from the right.

The school was much like modern schools except that discipline was much more strict. If the teachers didn't like what we were doing, they might hit us on the hand with a ruler. That stung!

Fun in Kindergarten

In the 1940s, kindergarten was more like preschool. We had lots of time to play and didn't work much on getting ready for first grade. We had music and art lessons and started to learn our letters for the next year.

My kindergarten class put on a show for our parents of the dances and songs we had learned. I did cartwheels and a somersault on stage. In this picture, you can see the pink dress I wore in the show.

I loved Miss Sleezer, my kindergarten teacher. She was pretty, soft-spoken, and gentle and loving. Here's a picture of her.

NAME _Gloria Kaszynski_ SCHOOL _Roosevelt_
TEACHER _Virginia Sleezer_ PERIOD ENDING _June 4, 1943_
HALF DAYS PRESENT _27_ HALF DAYS ABSENT _16_

MENTAL GROWTH
A. READING READINESS
  Gloria is ready for first grade reading.
B. PROBLEM SOLVING
  She very independently works out her own problems.
C. ORAL SELF EXPRESSION
  Gloria enjoys telling her interesting stories and she so enjoys a good joke.
D. CREATIVE SELF EXPRESSION
  Gloria is very original in expressing herself. Her art work is far above average. Her musical and rhythmic ability is excellent. She is graceful and creative in everything she does.

Miss Sleezer really liked me. In this report card, she wrote that Gloria "is creative in everything she does." Can you see how my last name has changed? It was Kaszynski before I was married.

Off to Catholic School

When I was in the third grade, my parents decided to send me to Saint Mary's, the local Catholic school. We were a very religious family, and it was important to my parents that I learn as much as I could about Catholicism.

Saint Mary's buildings were spread over a whole block and included the school, a big church, and a house for the priest. There was also a house

for the nuns who taught at the school and a social center for meetings and piano recitals. Open fields covered the rest of the land.

The classrooms were made with dark wood and were rather bare. I still remember their musty smell. Religious pictures and statues were displayed around each classroom to remind us how important religion was in our work and daily lives. The windows were very tall, and the teacher used a long pole with a knob at the end to open them at the top. There was no air conditioning, so by late spring, the breeze through the windows felt wonderful.

Class Equipment

You might have an overhead projector or a television and VCR in your classroom, but we didn't have those things in our day. We didn't even have a radio in our classroom.

We used our textbooks and the classroom chalkboard for all our lessons. Our textbooks were much older than the books we had used at Roosevelt School.

They were less colorful than the books you use. Our chalkboards were always black. It was an honor to be chosen to clean the chalkboards at the end of the day and to go outside to clap the dusty erasers together to clean them.

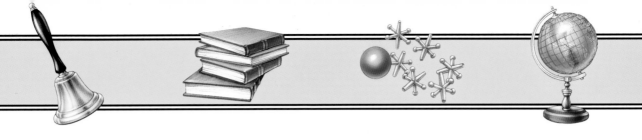

We sat in straight rows in desks with lids and inkwells on top. We wrote with number two pencils. At the top of all our papers we wrote "JMJ." Those are the initials of Jesus, Mary, and Joseph, the holy family of the Christian religion. Our teachers told us to ask for the holy family's help in all our schoolwork.

We weren't allowed to get up from our desks very much. The teacher always came to see us at our desks when we raised our hands. It was a relief to go to the back of the classroom to sharpen my pencil.

TICONDEROGA

A FINE AMERICAN PENCIL
WITH A FINE AMERICAN NAME

MADE IN U.S.A. DIXON TICONDEROGA 1386 N° 2

School Rules and Discipline

The Catholic school was more strict than the public school and had more rules. School began at nine o'clock. A nun rang a big brass bell, and we all lined up on the playground, with the youngest classes going first. Boys stood in one line and girls stood in another.

Our teachers were all nuns. We had to answer them formally, with "Yes, Sister," or "No, Sister." The sister put your name on the chalkboard if you were naughty and sometimes smacked your knuckles with a ruler. Naughty boys were sent to the cloakroom, where the coats were kept.

Several times each year, we had an assembly in the social center for the whole school. We started each assembly with the Pledge of Allegiance. For the spring assembly, we dressed in our best clothes and listened to the priest talk about the importance of Easter in the Catholic religion.

As in modern private schools, my parents had to pay a fee, called tuition, for me to attend a Catholic school. It was three dollars each month. Sometimes it was hard for my parents to afford the three dollars. Over the years, of course, school tuition has become much more expensive.

Mornings at Saint Mary's

Every morning, we began class with a prayer as we stood by our desks. Then we started work on our harder subjects—English, math, science, and geography. We learned many subjects by rote, or by memorizing and repeating facts. We never divided into smaller groups like you might do to work on different projects. We only worked in the classroom group.

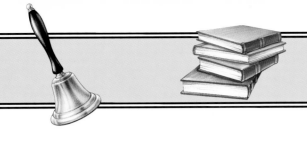

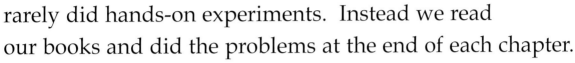

In your school, you might do science experiments with magnets, water, and clay. We rarely did hands-on experiments. Instead we read our books and did the problems at the end of each chapter.

It was really exciting in fourth grade when a boy in my class brought in the microscope kit he had received for Christmas. We each took turns looking through the eyepiece at a butterfly wing that had come with the kit. I had to squeeze one eye shut to see anything! I wrote a science report on how butterflies develop.

All of our classes at Saint Mary's had something to do with the Catholic religion. We read Bible stories to practice our reading and learned about the lives of saints. We practiced our math with religious problems, such as adding up different kinds of prayers. We also learned a lot about Bible history.

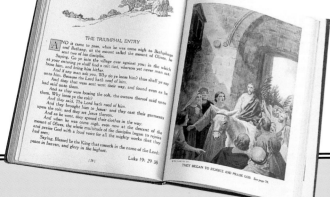

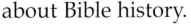

My Favorite Classes

I loved English, adored reading, and was especially good at diagramming sentences. That's taking a sentence apart and showing where the verbs, nouns, and prepositions are in the sentence.

In geography class, we learned the names of all the states in America, using a map that you had to put together like a jigsaw puzzle. We read *Scholastic* magazine, the same magazine you might read in your class.

For special assignments, we looked up information in the *National Geographic* magazines

at the back of the classroom. The magazines were usually two or three years old. Saint Mary's could not afford to buy them and depended on wealthier families to give the magazines to the classrooms.

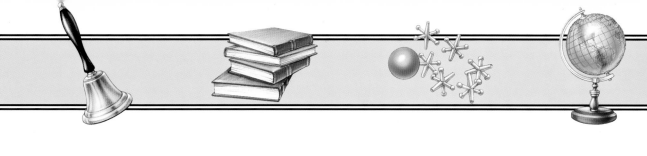

In history class, I was fascinated by the stories of the old sailing ships. These beautiful tall ships sped around the southern tip of South America and up the western coast of the United States, taking people to the gold rush in California. I imagined sailing the seas, captain of my own fast ship!

Lunch in the Classroom

We stayed in the classroom all day, except for recess after lunch. When a nun rang the bell, we all stood at our desks to say the Angelus prayer before we ate.

Lunch lasted one hour. Everyone brought a bag or pail lunch from home to eat at their desk. Most of

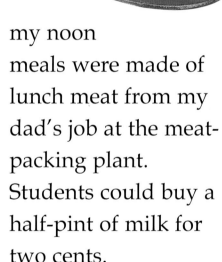

my noon meals were made of lunch meat from my dad's job at the meat-packing plant. Students could buy a half-pint of milk for two cents.

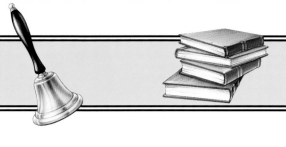

Sometimes during lunch, we visited the church, going in through the back door. We said a short prayer. The nuns would praise us for being religious. Sometimes they would give us special cards with saints on them.

ROSA MYSTICA

After lunch, we had recess in a large play area next to the school. This field was almost as big as half a city block, but there was very little equipment to play on. You can see the big field behind my fourth-grade classmates in the picture below.

Games at Recess

Most modern schools have sandboxes, swing sets, basketball hoops, and equipment with bridges, tunnels, slides, and bars to climb on and through. Our school had a small swing set with three seats and two baseball backstops.

We had no physical education classes. The only exercise we got was at recess, and we made up our own games. Kids often brought their own clotheslines from home to use as jump ropes. I loved jumping double Dutch, with two ropes going at the same time. We also played softball or swung on the old monkey bars with their sharp metal edges.

The girls played jacks, a game where we picked up small six-pointed metal toy pieces while we bounced a small ball on the ground. The boys played marbles. In this game, they tried to hit their friends' marbles out of a circle. I loved playing marbles and had my own bag of them, but the nuns wouldn't let me play. They said playing marbles wasn't suitable for girls.

Afternoon Classes

After lunch and recess, we had our writing class. Penmanship was very important to the teachers then. Most teachers in the 1940s taught a type of writing called Palmer penmanship. A diagram of the Palmer writing method ran across the front of classrooms.

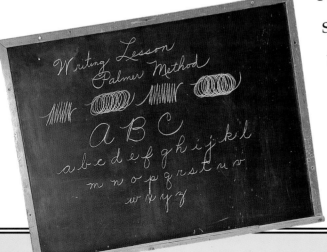

All the letters had to have smooth loops and slant to the right. Writing that way must have been really hard for left-handed children.

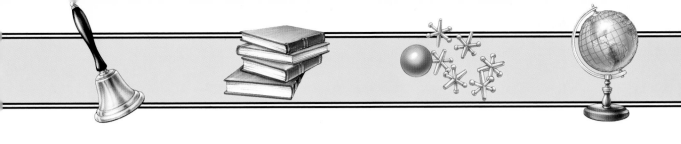

For writing class, we were allowed to write with fountain pens instead of our pencils. I felt so grown-up when I got my first fountain pen! A jar of ink came with it. The pen had a lever on the side that you pulled up on to suck ink from the jar. I had scratchy writing at first but soon learned to write smoothly.

For art class, the nuns would take a drawing from a coloring book and put it in the mimeograph machine to make copies. I felt important when I got to turn the handle on the mimeograph machine. We all colored the same picture. We were not supposed to make our own drawings or color outside the lines.

Piano Performance: A Big Event

In second grade, I started taking piano lessons at a nun's house before school. It cost one dollar for a half-hour lesson. (Even the least expensive piano lessons would cost your parents about twelve dollars.) Since we didn't have a piano at my house, I came early to practice for my lesson. My teacher would smack my fingers with a knitting needle if I made a mistake.

Every year in the spring, choral and piano recitals were held at the social center at school. About fifteen children each had one piece to perform that they had worked on all year. We were all very nervous. I was always frightened, but also excited.

Because I played piano well, I had two pieces every year— my piano solo and a duet with my friend Donna Benvenuti. One year, I got to perform my favorite song, "The Spinning Wheel."

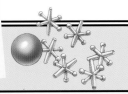

A Student Becomes a Teacher

After eighth grade, many of the children from my school went on to a Catholic school that was both a high school and a college. Two or three girls each year chose to go to Saint Joseph's Commercial, a business school that taught them how to be secretaries. The boys who thought they wanted to be priests went to Saint Bede's Academy.

The photo on the right shows my eighth-grade graduation, when I was fourteen. I'm first on the left in the

front row, and my best friend, Donna Benvenuti, is fourth from the right.

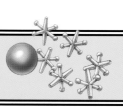

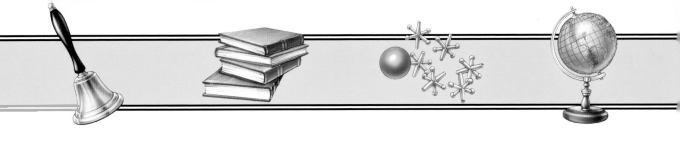

Girls were encouraged to be homemakers, nurses, teachers, or secretaries. There weren't many other choices. I grew up to become a mom and a teacher, using the things I had learned in school to teach children much like you!

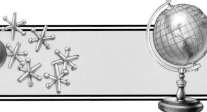

Glossary

assembly: a school meeting

cloakroom: a room where outdoor clothing is kept

crossing guard: a person who stops traffic so students can safely cross the street

fountain pen: a pen that must be filled with ink by hand

inkwell: a hole in a desk meant to hold a bottle of ink

mimeograph: a machine that presses ink through a stencil to make copies

penmanship: style of handwriting

recital: a concert given by music students

rote: learning by repetition

tuition: a fee paid to attend a private school

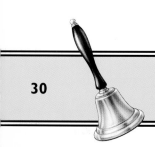

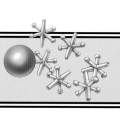

For Further Reading

Doney, Meryl. *Games.* New York: Franklin Watts, 1996.

Duden, Jane. *Timeline: 1940s.* New York: Crestwood House, 1989.

Rubel, David. *The United States in the 20th Century.* New York: Scholastic, 1995.

Stein, R. Conrad. *The Home Front.* Chicago: Children's Press, 1986.

Whitman, Sylvia. *V Is for Victory: The American Home Front during World War II.* Minneapolis, Minn.: Lerner Publications Co., 1993.

Illustrations are reproduced through the courtesy of: Gloria Jenkins, pp. 1, 4, 7, 8, 9 (top), 10 (left and right), 21 (top and bottom), 28; UPI/Corbis-Bettmann, pp. 5, 15; Archive Photos, pp. 6, 11, 14 (right), 24 (right); Corbis-Bettmann, pp. 13 (top), 23, 26; Robert Opie Collection, pp. 13 (bottom), 18 (right); Beamish Collection, p. 14 (left); Freelance Photographers Guild, p. 16; National Geographic, p. 18 (left); Scott Peterman/Devendra Shrikhande, p. 19; Stock Montage, p. 20 (left); Meeteetse Museums/Devendra Shrikhande, pp. 20 (right), 24 (left); Lambert/Archive Photos, p. 22.

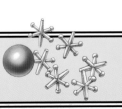

Index

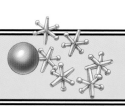